Heal Your Inner Child: A Guided Journal to Loving Yourself, Ending Self-Sabotage, and Changing Your Life

by Alegra Loewenstein

This book is dedicated to all of my health coaching clients. I am honored to have been your guide on this journey, and I always learned as much from you as you from me.

Table of Contents

Who is Your Inner Child?

YOUR INNER CHILD is the part of you that captured certain emotions and experiences in childhood and held onto them all these years. Though your adult mind is often unaware that your inner child still exists, he or she is inside you, and in a variety of ways may be trying to communicate with you.

What might this inner child be trying to say? We've been trained to ignore the requests of our inner child. There might be places or people that make you feel wrapped up in a warm hug. This is a sign that your inner child feels safe! Another clue is to look for anything, or anyone, that makes you giggle. If you have a friend who brings out your laughter, you can bet that your inner children are playing together!

There are many ways that we can begin to let this inner child out to play, and we can release all the laughter that comes along with him or her! Sometimes the idea of an inner child can be hard to conceptualize, but another way to think about this aspect of yourself is to consider the idea of having an inner puppy. Sometimes it's easier to dissociate further, and this in turn opens the door to association. If you had an inner puppy, wouldn't you want to let it out to play? Give it sunshine. Throw a ball for the puppy. Pet it and scratch its ears. Have fun!

You can also get in touch with your inner child in similar ways. You can get out some markers and an old pad of scratch paper, or pretty much any other art supplies. Color and draw, and throw them on the floor if you hate them, or even if you like them! Kids are often much more focused on the process of creating than on the finished product. Tap into that element of being in the moment for the sake of creating something, no matter how it turns out.

Play outside. Kids naturally want to run and jump on a play structure. Many adults have forgotten how, but you can cultivate this by giving yourself an obstacle course – can you race from one end to the next? Or find one of those outdoor fitness course circuits and do something on every station; you don't necessarily need to read the directions! Even just playing with a ball is an easy way to tap into the natural inclinations of your inner child. Do you want to throw it? Roll it? Kick it? Toss it? The possibilities are endless.

Have some fun remembering what your inner child likes to do, and have fun doing it. This is the first step to getting in touch with your inner child, and one we'll play around with in the prompts as well.

Why You Need to Heal Your Inner Child

HUMANS ARE COMPLEX CREATURES with a lot of social and emotional needs. We are also imperfect and prone to folly. This means that no matter your childhood experience, there were times when your loved ones and caregivers said or did things that scared you as a child. Now, as a child, there are certain basic needs that you need from your caregivers. Abandonment, whether physical or emotional, is a matter of life or death for a child. Therefore, fear of abandonment is one of the strongest feelings that a child can experience.

Additionally, the undeveloped child's mind can't reason that your loved one didn't mean it when he said, for example, he wished he could "go away and never come back." Likewise, even yelling or fighting between two adults might trigger a fear of abandonment that the child wants to control; in wishing to control your environment, you could have taken blame onto yourself for the fight, because if it's your fault, then you can do something about it.

However, as you eventually grow up and create your own independent life, these basic fears are no longer based on reality. While losing the love of a family member as a child could determine survival, as an adult it does not. (That is not to say broken relationships are not painful; they are – that is another matter.) Still, the imprint on your inner child remains, and when something happens in your life as an adult that makes you feel those same fears, it can keep you trapped in a pattern repeating fights and arguments that may no longer have any bearing on your life today.

The inner child is the part of you that did not receive the love that you wanted. Whether you came from a loving family or a broken or hurtful family, your inner child had needs that were not met. Your inner child is still asking you to meet those needs. Your inner child is still asking for your love today. This journal is designed to help you understand the cries of your inner child and learn to meet them, so you can feel safe and peaceful and break free of old patterns that no longer serve a purpose.

Your inner child may also simply want to play and be free! In our busy world, we often forget to nourish the playful part of our inner as well. From this perspective, your inner child is simply an aspect of your personality that may not be getting enough attention. This aspect of your inner child may not be wounded, but can still be a healing force in your life. As adults in today's world, we are often deprived of opportunities to play, and that in itself is a detriment to our health. By listening to the desires of your inner child, you will begin to find balance and relaxation as well, which also lends itself to a happier and healthier life as an adult.

How to Heal Your Inner Child

FOR THE PURPOSES of this journal, healing happens in two ways.

First, you find the wounds that your inner child still carries, and you heal those. This approach is more commonly talked about when you explore the world of the inner child. This is powerful work that can change how you feel and live in your day-to-day life. This approach is all about meeting the needs of your inner self, needs that can never be fully met by the outside world. Even the most loving parents cannot meet every need of the child. It is part of your spiritual evolution to learn to love yourself completely, to assure yourself that you will take care of yourself, and to give yourself the love you need from within. It is profound to love yourself deeply, to reassure yourself that you are complete and enough, no matter what fears you may have experienced about not being lovable or worthy of this love.

On the other side of the equation, you also have an opportunity to cultivate the innocence, playfulness, and curiosity of your inner child! When you cultivate your inner child, you may begin to ponder questions; you allow your mind to wander in ways you have likely forgotten how to do. You will dream and welcome those dreams into your life – without the adult tendency to judge or dismiss. You will again find the sense of wonder at the world around you that leaves you full of joy. Your creativity will be nourished. Your generosity will expand. Your sense of magic in the world will be rekindled. You will trust your heart and your soul will be inspired. If life circumstances caused you to lose this sense of wonder even earlier than most of us do, it is even more important that you create a sense of safety for your inner child, so that you can regain this profound wisdom.

There is no right or wrong way to complete this journal. While change will come faster with consistent, daily use, it's also okay to write less frequently or to take breaks. It's normal to get distracted, and it's fine to return to the work at any point.

1.   Ta-dah! Lists

There are three aspects of this journal. First, it's important to give yourself encouragement and build up your self-esteem. For most of us, our self-esteem was high as children, and unfortunately as society expresses pressure and judgment that confidence begins to fail as we grow into older children; our self-esteem drops dramatically in the teen years, and it takes a long time to recover. We can bolster our confidence and self-esteem by giving ourselves the praise that we need.

Sometimes we did not receive the praise we needed as children. Sometimes we received it, but our undeveloped minds doubted it. Sometimes we received it, but the mixed messages of society may have undermined it. It's never too late to observe and praise your own successes! This is one of the simplest and most powerful acts you can do to heal your self-esteem and grow your confidence. I call this your "Ta-dah! List," which is to counteract the adult tendency to give ourselves "To Do Lists" with no more praise than scratching it off when complete (and perhaps even feeling like we've never quite completed enough).

You can reverse engineer that tendency by writing down everything that you did well that day. It can be anything, from drinking a glass of water, to eating a piece of fruit, or staying calm when someone was getting angry, "using your words," having the courage to apologize to someone, sending an important email, playing with watercolors, receiving a postcard from a friend, giving or receiving a gift, or anything else that you feel proud or happy to have done that day! Think of this as a virtual high five to your inner child.

You can get printable copies of the Ta-dah! List at www.AlegraLoewenstien.com/heal-your-inner-child.

2.   Daily Prompts

Additionally, there are daily prompts. These take about five minutes to complete. Write anything that comes into your head, even if you digress from the initial prompt or question. Trust your subconscious mind. If you are thinking about something, it's important to write about it. The act of writing without judging or questioning in itself is a way to cultivate your inner child! Think about how children share stream of consciousness thoughts and ideas without fear! Let that part of you be free. It's as simple as putting pen to paper and writing until the page is filled.

3.   Reflection Pages

This is the trickiest step of them all. It's simple, and because it's the only step that happens off the pages of the journal, it may take longer to get the hang of it. Steps one and two are the practice run to help you start living step three in your day-to-day life. The reflection pages are designed to help you see how healing your inner child in the privacy of the pages of this journal are beginning to shift how your inner child behaves inside of you in the rest of your life. In other words, there will be times when you begin to realize that your actions now, as an adult, are actually actions that are being triggered by your inner child. As you begin to gain this awareness, you'll eventually be able to observe both your inner child and your adult self simultaneously, whereas before your inner child would take control without your adult self being aware of it. This is the path that will lead you from having heightened or dramatic reactions (the reactions of the child) to calmer, clearer actions. This is the way to awareness that you are safe, and your inner child is safe. This is also, thankfully, the path that allows you to let your inner child play more often and to be praised for doing so! Now, what child wouldn't want that?

The Journal

Ta Dah! What are some small (or large) things you did today that make you feel great?

____

____

____

____

____

Describe a comforting and fond memory from your childhood.

____

____

____

2

Ta Dah! What are some small (or large) things you did today that make you feel great?

____

____

____

____

____

Is there a physical act or item from yesterday's memory that you could use in your life now?

For example, sliced apples that remind you of how your mother gave you sliced apples when you were sick, the cup of chamomile tea served before bedtime, your love of playing catch, or the joy of looking up at clouds and treetops.

____

____

____

____

____

____

____

____

Brainstorm ways that you can give your inner child a chance to enjoy this act or item in your life now.

For example, giving yourself the gift of slicing the apple before eating it, making yourself that cup of chamomile tea, finding someone to play catch with, or just lying down to look up at the sky.

Ta Dah! What are some small (or large) things you did today that make you feel great?

____

____

____

____

____

What makes you whine (or at least makes you want to whine)?

____

____

____

____

Whining is a telltale sign your inner child
needs something. What could it be?

Ta Dah! What are some small (or large) things you did today that make you feel great?

____

____

____

____

____

What were your favorite games and activities as a child?

____

____

____

____

____

Can you find a way to play some of these
now?

Ta Dah! What are some small (or large) things you did today that make you feel great?

____

____

____

____

What do you complain about?

____

____

____

____

Relate this complaint back to what your inner child might need. The answer to this might be how your inner child is telling you: "I feel neglected," or "I'll never succeed." Remember, the negative feelings of the inner child are based on fear and survival instinct; they are thoughts created by an undeveloped mind. They may have been valuable at some point in time; now you are safe, and you can begin to recognize and transform them.

____

____

____

____

____

____

____

Ta Dah! What are some small (or large) things you did today that make you feel great?

____

____

____

____

____

Spend a few minutes meditating on the emotions that may have come up from yesterday's journal entry. When we complain, we are often covering up deeper emotions like anger or sadness. By allowing yourself the opportunity to feel the range of emotions associated with the things you complain about without trying to stop it or push it down, you will learn that all your emotions are safe to feel. This, in turn, teaches your inner child that the world is

safe and that you are there to protect him or her.
Feel free to write down anything you observed when you allowed yourself to feel these emotions.

____

____

____

____

____

____

____

____

____

____

Ta Dah! What are some small (or large) things you did today that make you feel great?

____

____

____

____

____

Write down some of the personality traits from your childhood that you love about yourself. Perhaps you loved to tell jokes, were a fashionista, were really good at building towers, or drew chalk murals. You can think of what you adore about your childhood self – anything goes!

____

8

Ta Dah! What are some small (or large) things you did today that make you feel great?

____

____

____

____

____

____

Look back at yesterday's list of fun and fabulous traits of your childhood self. Are there ways you can re-cultivate any of those now? You can recreate them exactly, for example, by breaking out the chalk and having some fun drawing, or you can reinterpret them in a more adult way, perhaps by spending some time making your wardrobe more fresh, fun, or funky.

Reflection Pages

It's time to put on your observer hat. Whether this means you pretend to be a sociologist, psychologist, therapist, scientist, social worker, life coach, anthropologist, or anything else, you start by getting yourself ready to observe. That means you must set the judgment aside.

Look back on the past few days (or week) and ask yourself if there was a time that your emotional reaction made you react disproportionately greater (got more upset at the time than may seem warranted in retrospect). This is the sign that your inner child was involved. Simply write down what was happening. Who were you with? What was happening?

____

____

____

Review your initial description. If you use language that is full of judgment, rewrite your observations now, without judgment. That includes removing the words "should have" or "shouldn't have." Also, any time you use "why," it should come from a place of true curiosity (not a rhetorical question that is really just blaming yourself).

____

____

____

____

____

____

____

____

____

Ta Dah! What are some small (or large) things you did today that make you feel great?

It is impossible to truly understand what a newborn child feels and experiences. To be sure, it must be a bombardment of experiences and feelings that only someday will evolve into true emotions. Take a few moments now to give your inner child the gift of a warm and loving welcome into this world. Imagine yourself being born. This can be how you know you were born, or how you imagine or wish you were born. Now your physical adult self should gather up your imaginary newborn self into your arms and hold and love your newborn self with kind and loving thoughts, words, feelings, and emotions. Pour all your love from your adult self into your newborn self. Tell your newborn self all the ways you will love and protect him or her in this crazy world we live in.

Afterwards, write down any observations about this meditation.

____

____

____

____

____

____

____

____

Ta Dah! What are some small (or large) things you did today that make you feel great?

____

____

____

____

What makes you mad? Really mad?

____

____

____

____

____

____

____

____

____

____

____

____

The answer to this might be how your inner child is telling you, "I'm afraid" or "I'm not good enough." Remember, the negative feelings of the inner child are based on fear and survival instinct; they are thoughts created by an undeveloped mind. They may have been valuable at some point in time; now you are safe, and you can begin to recognize and transform them.

Ta Dah! What are some small (or large) things you did today that make you feel great?

____

____

____

____

____

Often one of the earliest emotions that a child learns to express is that of anger. Perhaps this is the reason that anger also remains one of the most widespread and lingering emotions as an adult. This means that the feeling of anger often covers other emotions like a blanket, making it difficult to recognize, identify, and describe the true emotions underneath that anger. Take some time now to explore the things that make you mad and try to expand the emotions behind these triggers. If your inner child had words to explicitly express the true fear-driven emotions, what might it be?

For example, my own inner child is very often made to "feel small." This might come across as feeling unimportant, or unheard, or any other number of expressions, all of which make me very mad. By recognizing the wider expression, I can speak to my inner child and bolster her up, explaining that sometimes we don't get heard, but what she has to say is still important!

____

____

____

____

____

____

____

____

Ta Dah! What are some small (or large) things you did today that make you feel great?

____

____

____

____

____

All children need to play, and your inner child needs time to play as well. In what ways are you (or can you be) playful in your life now?

____

____

____

____

Unfortunately, the modern world does not value time to play. It might not be easy to give yourself the gift of play. Come up with some fun, simple ways that you can be more playful. Here is a list to help you get started; be sure to add more to it.

Doodle
Draw
Write a poem
Lie in the grass
Log roll down a hill
Start a collection
Walk aimlessly
Drive aimlessly
Tell a joke
Play a prank
Watch a comedy
Send a postcard

____

____

____

____

____

Ta Dah! What are some small (or large) things you did today that make you feel great?

____

____

____

____

____

This guided meditation is designed to help you deal with the emotions and situations that make you feel "triggered." Feeling triggered is a general term that means you have an intense and negative emotional reaction. Feeling triggered is a sure sign that your inner child is in reaction and taking over your adult mind. If you have more than one way you feel triggered, choose one type of triggered feeling for this meditation (anger, frustration, annoyance, etc.).

Spend a few minutes going back in time in your mind to find a time in your life when you had never felt this feeling before. This memory can be real or made up. If nothing is coming to you, go into your time as a baby, into the womb. If still no memory comes that is free and clear of ever having felt triggered, go into a past life. It doesn't matter if you don't believe in past lives (I don't); this is just a way to store a memory or feeling. Keep going back and back in time until you find a memory, any memory, in which you had never felt this triggered emotion.

Write down this memory, whether real or imagined.

____

____

____

____

____

____

____

____

____

____

____

____

____

____

Having this memory available to you will help you deal with the triggered emotions when they happen in your daily life. Now you have a time to recall in which you had never felt this way, which will empower you to stay calm even when the emotions arise.

15

Ta Dah! What are some small (or large) things you did today that make you feel great?

Spend some time contemplating life's big questions with a sense of awe and wonder – the sense of a child.

Recall a concept from your childhood that felt so expansive or infinite that you could not comprehend it. Remember how this felt. Did it feel awe-inspiring? Did it feel frustrating? Did it feel exciting? Scary?

For example, I remember wanting to know where space ends. While it felt frustrating to me as a child to have an unanswerable question, I can now view that same unanswerable question with a sense of wonder. In this way, I can actually feel more in touch with my inner child as an adult than I did back then.

____

____

____

____

____

____

____

____

____

16

Ta Dah! What are some small (or large) things you did today that make you feel great?

____

____

____

____

What makes you cry?

____

____

____

____

———————————————————

———————————————————

———————————————————

———————————————————

———————————————————

———————————————————

———————————————————

———————————————————

The answer to this might be how your inner child is telling you: "I feel abandoned" or "I'm scared." Remember, the negative feelings of the inner child are based on fear and survival instinct; they are thoughts created by an undeveloped mind. They may have been valuable at some point in time; now you are safe, and you can begin to recognize and transform them.

Ta Dah! What are some small (or large) things you did today that make you feel great?

____

____

____

____

____

Spend a few minutes to meditate on the sadness from yesterday's journal entry. It is scary to feel sad. If it is helpful, talk to your inner child. Tell your inner child: "I know you are sad. I am here to keep you safe. I love you even when you are sad." By allowing yourself the opportunity to feel this sadness without trying to stop it or push it down, you will learn that all your emotions are safe to feel. This, in turn, teaches your inner child that the world is safe, and that you are there to protect him or her.

Feel free to write down anything you observed when you allowed yourself to feel these emotions.

Ta Dah! What are some small (or large) things you did today that make you feel great?

____

____

____

____

Consider your inner child the hero from a story. Now write a scene from that story! What happens to the little you? What adventures does he or she go on?

____

____

____

____

Reflection Pages

Just like last time, put aside judgment. If it helps to pretend to be in the role of an official observer, imagine yourself in that role (sociologist, psychologist, etc.).

For this reflection, notice any times in the past few days (or week) when you did something differently from what you normally do.

- Did you allow yourself to take a nap?
- Did you change the subject of a long-standing argument?
- Did you walk away from a negative situation you usually stay involved in?
- Did you take a deep breath before saying something?
- Did you take a deep breath at all?
- Did you sit and watch the clouds?
- Did you make a mental plan before bringing a concern up with someone?
- Did you go for an aimless walk?
- Did you avoid a stressful situation?

- Did you handle stress better?

Find any change in your behavior or reaction that is different from how you've done things before. It takes time to do things the right way, but the hardest thing is to NOT do things the old way, so it's worthwhile to observe and celebrate any change!

____

____

____

____

____

____

____

____

____

Review your initial description. If you use language that is full of judgment, rewrite your observations now, without judgment. That includes removing the words "should have" or "shouldn't have."

____

____

____

____

____

____

____

____

____

Ta Dah! What are some small (or large) things you did today that make you feel great?

____

____

____

____

In what ways do you demand attention from those around you?

____

____

____

____

____

____

____

____

____

____

____

____

The answer to this might be how your inner child is telling you: "What I have to say doesn't matter" or "Please notice me." Remember, the negative feelings of the inner child are based on fear and survival instinct; they are thoughts created by an undeveloped mind. They may have been valuable at some point in time; now you are safe, and you can begin to recognize and transform them.

Ta Dah! What are some small (or large) things you did today that make you feel great?

____

____

____

____

____

When you try to demand attention from someone, what happens? Does it draw you together or push you apart? Does it give you the feeling or satisfaction you are craving, or not?

____

____

____

____

Ta Dah! What are some small (or large) things you did today that make you feel great?

____

____

____

____

____

We tend to be hardest on ourselves. Write down some ways that you are hard on yourself. If possible, write down the exact thoughts. Some common areas are in expecting perfection in career performance, demanding unrealistic limits on what you eat, degrading your own body, or blaming yourself for not creating a desired result in your personal or social life.

Now take a moment to rewrite each of the comments into a kind comment. Imagine you are talking to your inner child.

Examples:
- *"This document is terrible." -> "You did your best, and you can feel proud to turn that in today."*
- *"I was so bad today." -> "You overate. Let's have some tea and go to bed early."*
- *"I look disgusting." -> "That color makes your eyes look great!"*
- *"Why can't I make that person do that thing?" -> "You are working hard to improve yourself."*

____

____

____

____

____

____

Ta Dah! What are some small (or large) things you did today that make you feel great?

____

____

____

____

____

We come into this world hungry, and we still have a hunger. It may not be for milk anymore, but it is for nourishment for the soul. We can feed this newborn child in the inner realm and satisfy this need.

Try this simple meditation. Shut your eyes, and imagine yourself as a baby, just born into this world, crying for your basic needs. Now, imagine your adult self as feeding this baby self. This might be a literal feeding of the baby through breast or bottle, or it might be an imaginative feeding through word, image, thought, or feeling. However you imagine, it is the right way. Imagine you feed and nourish this baby version of yourself, giving it the love and sustenance it needs to feel calm, safe, and happy.

Write down any thoughts or feelings that may have arisen during this meditation.

Ta Dah! What are some small (or large) things you did today that make you feel great?

____

____

____

____

____

The idea of summer has an innate aspect of childhood in it. The long daylight hours entice us to stay up past our bedtime. The school days seem so far off that it feels like forever. Write down a memory (from any age) of a time when you felt totally footloose and fancy free.

____

____

Ta Dah! What are some small (or large) things you did today that make you feel great?

Create a timeline of your life (as best you can) from the ages of about three years old until about seven years old.

Many of our inner child wounds are created at around age five or six. This is the time when our brains are developed enough to apply logic, but that logic still doesn't make sense. This combination means that we become convinced that our strong emotional reactions (such as fear or rejection) are caused by our own flaws. This might mean we feel unlovable, or afraid of intimacy, or rejected by those closest to us, or fearful, or anxious, or any other number of negative emotions. Create a map or timeline of stress factors that may have been happening in your life at this tender age. Doing this simple assessment can give your adult mind a chance to reflect on possible deep-rooted emotions that were created at that time.

If you don't know, or if nothing seems stressful, that's okay, too. You can write down any memory from this time that may feel significant.

For example, I remember a time in gym class when the whole class was acting up, led by the boys, but only I got in trouble. In my mind, the PE coach was singling me out against the boys, and it created a feeling in my stomach that is the same as whenever I feel like I'm "in trouble" even to this day. Remembering this as an early version of that feeling gives me the insight to know that some of my inner child reaction is based on feeling singled out by the men in charge.

Ta Dah! What are some small (or large) things you did today that make you feel great?

____

____

____

____

What aspects of your life need more fun and playfulness?

____

____

____

____

Ta Dah! What are some small (or large) things you did today that make you feel great?

____

____

____

____

Write a letter to your inner child. Tell him or her that you understand what he or she is experiencing, and that you are here to support him or her through the big emotions. Pledge your love and attention to your inner child in this letter.

Dear ______________,

Ta Dah! What are some small (or large) things you did today that make you feel great?

____

____

____

____

____

It's time to envision the way you want your inner child to feel all the time. For this prompt, you can write down a real memory or you can make one up. You can even rewrite a real memory to make it better!

Describe a happy scene when your inner child felt fully loved and appreciated. Make this the perfect memory, full of feelings of love and confidence. This is the gift of childhood that you can give your inner child at any time, simply by remembering this perfect "memory."

Reflection Pages

Just like last time, put aside judgment. If it helps to pretend to be in the role of an official observer, imagine yourself in that role.

Here are some examples of things that are worth noting:

- Was there a time when you honored what your inner child needed?
- Was there a time you allowed your inner child to come out and play?
- Was there a time when, in the heat of the moment (feeling triggered), you were able to recognize your reaction as the exaggerated reaction of your inner child? (Even if no actions changed, just observing this is proof of heightened awareness!)
- Was there a time when you took a new action that honored the needs of both your adult self and inner child?

Look back over the past few days or week and find baby steps that you've taken "in the moment" that are worthy of praise. These can be very small changes. Even just becoming more aware of your triggers is an important change.

____

____

____

____

____

____

____

____

____

Keep this list (and all the other observations, reflections, and explorations you've done in this journal) and refer back to it periodically to continue to heal your inner child, love yourself, end self-sabotage, and change your life!

About the Author

Alegra Loewenstein is a best-selling author, speaker, and coach on the topics of holistic health, emotional eating, and how an earth-based spirituality can foster health and happiness.

Through her coaching, e-courses, and books, she helps people to lose weight in a safe and sustained way without dieting or deprivation, by following the practice of the Wheel of the Year. Her recent *Food Journal Magic* is designed to do exactly this, while *Kitchen Magic* brings a mindset of abundance to your kitchen and health.

She is also the author of two best-selling guided journals, including *Emotional Eating Detox* and *Body Wisdom Journal*.

Alegra inspires busy, ambitious leaders to slow down, tune in to their holistic whole body, connect to their desires, cultivate their intuition, and lose weight with ease. This simple, sustainable approach brings work-life balance and leads to greater success.

Alegra's passion is guiding us back to enjoying and actually living life in the midst of our hectic, full schedules.

She likes tea, chocolate, and reading self-help books. Alegra lives in sunny San Diego with her boys, where she writes and creates amongst cacti, coyotes, and wildflowers.

www.AlegraLoewenstein.com/freegift

Books by the Author

Emotional Eating Detox: A 21-Day Inspirational Journal to Understand Your Cravings, End Overeating, and Find Freedom from Dieting Forever

Body Wisdom Journal: 40 Days to Heal & Listen to Your Body's Intuition

Kitchen Magic: Simple Recipes & Rituals to Manifest Health & Happiness

Food Journal Magic: A Daily Food & Fitness Diary to Create Lasting Weight Loss That Stays Off Without a Diet

It's Not About the Food: Personal Stories and Inspiration from Health Coaches and Wellness Experts to Transform Your Weight Loss Mindset and Lose Weight without a Diet

Too Busy to Cook: Your Guide to Meal Planning and Food Prep that is Twice as Healthy in Half the Time

Acknowledgements

I thank **my mom**! She is a naturally Zen and balanced person, and I will always be inspired by her.

I also thank **my dad** for always being generous and supportive.

Thank you to **Marshall**, for being patient as I grow my dreams into reality. Nothing makes me prouder than when our kids describe my work as writing and helping people.

I am also deeply grateful for the love and support of all my family, especially **Aurora**, **Seren**, **Linda**, **Marla**, **Katie**, **Sarah**, and **Ted**. Thanks for reading, asking questions, and being enthusiastic.

A few ideas in this book were particularly inspired by conversations with my friend, mentor, and unofficial fairy goddess/mother, **Mysti**. I'm so grateful for our friendship and your wisdom!

Thank you to my improv teacher, **Jacquie Lowell**, who was the very first reader of this book!

Finally, I acknowledge the work I did with **Lorraine Cohen**. Her expertise in inner child work influenced my approach to this book. May she go towards the light.

www.ingramcontent.com/pod-product-compliance
Lightning Source LLC
Chambersburg PA
CBHW020528160726
47992CB00005BA/2293